Plastic Planet

Georgia Amson-Bradshaw

W

First published in Great Britain in paperback in 2020 by the Watts Publishing Group
Copyright © the Watts Publishing Group 2019

Editor: Georgia Amson-Bradshaw
Designer: Rocket Design (East Anglia) Ltd

Getty Images: Carol Buchanan/age fotostock: 21br, 45br; Debbi Smimoff; 29t; VCG: 16bl. iStockphoto: gemreddin: 22b. NOAA: Claire Fackler, CINMS: 24bl. Shutterstock: Abscent: 18bl; Adlike: 5b; Akvaartist: 16tc; Almazova: 19t; Artography: 39b; Azaze11o: 12br; bioraven: 29b, 46bl; Blue Ring Media: 14bc, 15bl, 15br, 33cr; branding as hell: 39t; Bubbers BB: 35tr; Nadia Buravleva: 38r; Rich Carey: 21t; Jose Luis Carrascosa: 37tr; createvil: 22cl; Creative mood: 26b; daewoosao: 12bc; Zaytseva Darya: 31c, 45t; Drawii: 5bc; Le Do: 37br; elic: 20bg; EniaB: 30cr; foxie: 11cl; Foxyliam: 13bl; Stuart Fuidge: 10bc, 44bl; Elena Garder: 7tr; gentlemanrook/CC Wikimedia Commons: 6b; Green Angel: 16-17c; grivka: 24b; gst: 2,7cl, 22cr, 47tr; Mary Hat: 7tl; In-finity: 7b; Jamesbin: 14t, 15c; Zmiciier Kavabata: 43t; kilkavbanke: 21b, 25br; Laia Design Lab: 28b; Lexamer: 11tr; Ksenia Lokko: 36l; LuminoOne: 38b; Marie Maerz: 30b; Makc: 7trb; malinka: 23tr; Merggy: 34; mirrelley: 23b; More Vector: 8bl; Mr Lightman 1975: 11cr; Nevodka: 4c; NotionPic: 32b; Olga 1818 : 30l; Olha1981: 20c; Orakunyab: 41b; Yauhen Paleski: 13tr; Papakah: 27b; patrimonio designs ltd: 9tl; peroni: 1; petovarga: 14bl; Irena Peziene: 9b; W. Phokin: 38-39bg; Photokup: 34cr; pikepicture: 11br; Pixotico: 40b; Olga Pogorelova: 3t,11tl, 20l, 21r; Irina Qiwi: 12bl; rawpixel: 32t; ReachDreams: 19b; Redcollegiya: 42bg; RedlineVector: 43b; Rvector: 11bl; Sarunyu_foto: 40t; Alexey Seafarer: 24-25t; Shtefany: 39c; Sidhe: 7cr; Sketch Master: 13br; Roman Sotola: 33cl;StockSmartStart: 16-17 frame; Studio Wiki: 5t; studioworkstock: 21c; Sudowoodo:33br; Rinat Sultanov: 9tc,35bl;48b; Supriya07: 25bl, 46br; KY Tan: 18tr; Tarikdiz: 37cl; tele52: 9tr; The Fisherman: 26t, 27t; Tribalum: 33 symbols; Tonis Valing: 28c; Duda Vasilii: 33bl; Vectors Bang: 33tl; Vectorpocket: 17cr, 33tr; Vimos Virgo: 8br; Vixenchristy: 34; Vlada Art: 3bl, 17tl, 45bl; Dirk Wahn:18-19 bg; Holla Wise: 3br, 31b; Alien Zagrebeinaya: 20bl, 25cr. The Ocean Cleanup: 42t. Wikimedia Commons: Permission of Science History Institute/PDS: 10bl.

ISBN: 978 1 4451 6570 7

Printed in Dubai

Franklin Watts
An imprint of
Hachette Children's Group
Part of the Watts Publishing Group
Carmelite House
50 Victoria Embankment
London EC4Y 0DZ

An Hachette UK Company
www.hachette.co.uk
www.franklinwatts.co.uk

CONTENTS

THE PLASTIC PROBLEM 4

WHAT IS PLASTIC? 6

INVENTING PLASTIC 8

CASE STUDY: BAKELITE 10

HOW WE USE PLASTIC 12

WHERE PLASTIC GOES 14

CASE STUDY: YANGTZE RIVER, CHINA ... 16

MICROPLASTICS 18

CASE STUDY: PACIFIC GARBAGE PATCH .. 20

IMPACT ON WILDLIFE 22

CASE STUDY: ALBATROSS 24

IMPACT ON HUMANS 26

WHAT IS BEING DONE? 28

WHAT CAN YOU DO? 30

RECYCLING PLASTIC 32

WHAT ABOUT BIOPLASTIC? 34

A PLASTIC-FREE KITCHEN 36

A PLASTIC-FREE BATHROOM 38

SPREAD THE WORD 40

SCIENTIFIC SOLUTIONS 42

GLOSSARY 44

FURTHER READING 46

INDEX 48

BAN SINGLE-
USE PLASTICS
NOW!

ACT
NOW!

BAD
PLASTIC

THE PLASTIC PROBLEM

Look around you, and you'll almost certainly be able to see something made of plastic. It's an incredibly useful material, but the way we have been using and disposing of plastic around the world is causing huge problems.

HERE FOREVER

One of the great benefits of plastic is that it doesn't break down. But this is one of its biggest drawbacks, too. When plastic gets into the environment, such as into the oceans and the landscape, it can stay there for thousands of years, causing long-lasting pollution.

A million plastic bottles are bought around the world **EVERY MINUTE** – that's 20,000 a second – and demand is increasing every year.

Turtles die when they eat plastic which they mistake for jellyfish.

SINGLE-USE PLASTIC

Although plastic takes a long time to decompose, we often treat it like a throw-away material. Around half of the plastic produced each year is turned into single-use items, such as drinks bottles, takeaway cutlery, straws and food wrappers that get used once and then thrown away.

When you consider that a plastic fork might last several centuries, it seems ridiculous to only use it for a few minutes, then throw it in the bin!

PLASTIC IN THE OCEAN

Up to 12.7 million tonnes of plastic is ending up as waste in the ocean each year (read more about how this happens on pages 16 and 17). This plastic pollution is having devastating impacts on the ocean's wildlife, killing over a hundred million marine animals each year, and it may be causing harm to our health too. Plastic has become a monster of a problem – read on to find out how we got here, and what we can do to solve it.

If nothing changes, by 2050 there will be more plastic by weight in the ocean than fish.

What IS plastic?

The word 'plastic' means something that can be easily shaped or moulded. When plastic was invented, its amazing versatility is partly what earned it the nickname 'the wonder material'. But what actually is it?

POLYMER

Plastic is a man-made material, or rather, materials, because there are lots of different types. They are all referred to scientifically as polymers. A polymer is a very large molecule, made up of lots of smaller molecules that are joined together in a very long chain.

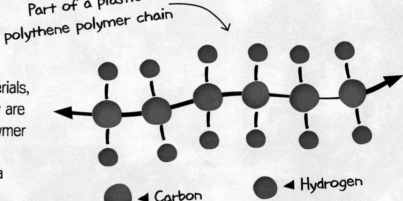

Part of a plastic polythene polymer chain

◄ Carbon   ◄ Hydrogen

Newly-made plastic is supplied in the form of powders or 'nurdles', small pellets of plastic, to the factories that produce plastic objects.

CRUDE OIL

The raw material for most plastic is crude oil, a fossil fuel that forms underground over millions of years. The oil is processed, then mixed with chemicals called catalysts, which kick-start a chemical reaction called polymerisation. This creates the basic substance which can then be used to make different plastic items.

PROPERTIES OF PLASTIC

MOULDABLE
It can be made into any shape you want.

LIGHT AND STRONG
It weighs very little for how strong it is, compared to materials such as wood or glass.

WATERPROOF
It doesn't let water through it, which makes it useful for keeping food fresh.

VERSATILE
It can be clear or coloured, and can be made into lots of different textures.

ADDICTED to PLASTIC

With all these handy qualities, it's not surprising that plastic has quickly become an important part of our lives. But we need to solve the problem of our dependency on it. As well as causing serious ocean pollution, the plastic-making process releases the gas carbon dioxide (CO_2), which contributes to climate change. On top of this, crude oil is a finite resource, meaning it will one day run out. For all these reasons, we need to rethink our reliance on plastic.

Oil refineries, where crude oil is processed, release a lot of CO_2.

INVENTING PLASTIC

Plastic is a relatively new invention. It didn't become really widespread until the middle of the 20th century, but scientists and engineers are working on new types all the time.

FANTASTIC PLASTIC TIMELINE

THE FIRST PLASTIC

Alexander Parkes, from Birmingham in the UK, creates the first 'plastic' from cellulose and camphor, natural substances from plants.

1869

1907

1855

ARTIFICIAL IVORY

A shortage of ivory for billiard balls prompts a New York company to offer US $10,000 to anyone who can make a replacement. John Wesley Hyatt develops Parkes' method and creates celluloid, the first artificial plastic.

BAKELITE

The first synthetic plastic (made from chemicals, instead of natural materials) is Bakelite, made by Leo Baekeland (see p.10–11). It is used for household objects.

NYLON

Making plastic into fabric, instead of solid objects, is explored by the American company Du Pont. In 1935, one of the chemists there develops nylon, an artificial silk. One of its first major uses is for parachutes during the Second World War (1939–1945).

FLYING PLASTICS

The 21st century sees even more types of plastic developed, for even more applications. In 2009, the new Boeing 787 aeroplane is made of 50 per cent plastic.

VEGGIE-PLASTIC

British company ICI launches Biopol, the first biodegradeable plastic made from sweet potatoes, peas and other vegetable starches

1935

1965

1990

2009

KEVLAR

Polish-American chemist Stephanie Kwolek invents Kevlar, a plastic that for its weight is five times stronger than steel. First used in racing tyres, it has many applications, including bulletproof vests and undersea cables.

THE FUTURE

Scientists are still working on new types of plastic, from self-healing plastics that repair themselves when they are damaged, to plastics made from corn that break down and so don't cause pollution (read about this on pages 34 and 35).

BAKELITE

The first synthetic plastic, Bakelite, was advertised as 'the material with 1,000 uses'. In fact, this turned out to be an underestimate!

LEO BAEKELAND (1863–1944)

Bakelite's inventor was Belgian-American chemist, Leo Baekeland. He was already rich before inventing Bakelite, having invented a type of photographic paper, the rights to which he sold in 1899 for US $1,000,000 - nearly US $30,000,000 today. With his fortune, he built a high-tech research lab in his own home to develop more inventions.

A Bakelizer from Baekeland's lab, for making Bakelite.

SHELLAC REPLACEMENT

Baekeland set about trying to make a synthetic replacement for natural shellac, which was used to insulate electrical wires. He experimented with applying heat and pressure to the chemicals phenol and formaldehyde, creating Bakelite.

Shellac is produced by the female lac bug, from south Asia. It is still used today to glaze furniture, and on sweets to make them shiny!

Properties of Bakelite

Bakelite had many of the properties which are so useful in modern plastics. It was easily mouldable, heat-resistant, did not conduct electricity, had a smooth texture and could be produced in many colours.

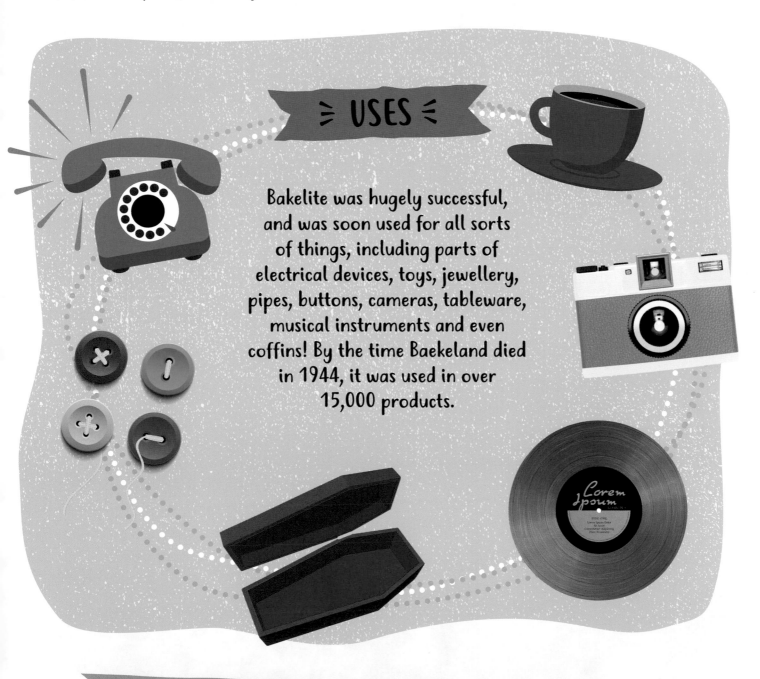

⇒ USES ⇒

Bakelite was hugely successful, and was soon used for all sorts of things, including parts of electrical devices, toys, jewellery, pipes, buttons, cameras, tableware, musical instruments and even coffins! By the time Baekeland died in 1944, it was used in over 15,000 products.

After bakelite

By the late 1940s, Bakelite had begun to be overtaken by newer types of plastic which were cheaper to make and less brittle.

HOW WE USE PLASTIC

Today, there is hardly any area of life in which plastic isn't used. From the moment we get up, to the moment we go to bed, we use plastic objects all day long.

 7.30 AM

 8.00 AM

 9.00 AM

WAKEY WAKEY

When we wake up, we clean our teeth. Toothbrushes and toothpaste tubes are made of plastic — but very few of them are recyclable. Every toothbrush you have ever used is almost certainly lying in a landfill dump somewhere right now.

GETTING DRESSED

The most popular fibre for making clothes with is polyester, a type of plastic. It can be made into many different textures, and is cheap to produce, making it ideal for our throwaway culture where clothes are often bought, worn for a short period of time, and then disposed of.

GOING TO SCHOOL

After a breakfast of milk from a plastic bottle and cereal from a plastic bag, we head off to school or work. Inside the car or bus, the panels are plastic. At school, we use plastic pens, eat plastic-wrapped snacks and play with plastic balls at break time.

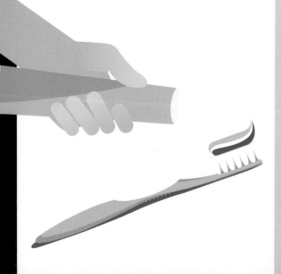

OUT IN SPACE

It isn't just everyday life which is dominated by plastic. Out in space, astronauts work in spaceships made with plastic. In hospitals, plastic instruments are used to treat patients. Plastic is used in lots of cutting-edge scientific processes.

 5.00 PM

IN THE EVENING

After school and work, we relax in front of the TV or play on phones and tablets – all with plastic components. We sit on furniture with plastic frames, covered with plastic-based fabric, before maybe having a bath with shampoo from a plastic bottle, and going to bed.

NASA scientists have developed a material made of old plastic bags that's even stronger and lighter than aluminium. It could be used to protect spaceships travelling to Mars from space debris.

BEFORE PLASTIC

Over time, plastic has come to replace more and more of the materials that were used in the past. But we could go back to using other materials more, such as paper, glass or tin for food packaging and cotton or wool for clothes. Would you use a toothbrush of pig bristles?

WHERE PLASTIC GOES

Shockingly, of the 300 million tonnes of plastic produced every year, worldwide only around 10 per cent is recycled. So where is all this plastic going?

LANDFILL

The amount of plastic that gets recycled varies around the world. In Europe, 30 per cent of plastic waste is recycled, whereas in the US it's only 9 per cent – and even this figure may not be accurate, as some of it is recycled abroad (see below). All around the world, the majority is simply sent to landfill: big holes in the ground filled with rubbish.

BURNING

In some countries, such as Sweden, plastic waste is burnt in power plants to produce energy. This has the benefit of not releasing plastic rubbish into the environment, but it produces a lot of air pollution and greenhouse gases, and doesn't conserve materials in the way that recycling does.

Landfills are filling up. The USA could run out of landfill space in 18 years.

Until recently, half of plastic waste from the USA and one third from the European Union was sent to China to be recycled.

WHY ARE RECYCLING RATES SO LOW?

The low levels of plastic recycling are down to a few factors. Even in countries that have good waste collection and sorting systems, it is difficult and expensive to sort the many different types of plastic which all need to be recycled separately. Because new plastic is so cheap to produce, it's often more expensive to recycle than to simply make new.

WOAH!
A plastic bottle can take 450 years to break down.

POLLUTION

The other place that waste plastic goes is out into the environment. In many less developed countries, the waste collection and recycling systems aren't very efficient, so people dispose of their rubbish by dumping it on the land or throwing it into waterways. This is the main source of plastic that ends up in the ocean, as it gets washed down the waterways into the sea.

YANGTZE RIVER, CHINA

Plastic in the ocean mostly comes down through rivers in areas that have poor waste management systems. In fact, ten river systems account for 90 per cent of the plastic in the ocean, and the Yangtze in China is the largest contributor of all.

FACT FILE

Length: **6,300 km**

Population around the river: **400 million**

Plastic deposited in ocean: **1.5 million tonnes per year**

NO WASTE MANAGEMENT

The Yangtze flows though some of China's most densely populated areas, including the city of Shanghai with 22 million inhabitants. Along the river's length millions of people live without proper waste management systems, and the river is where a lot of the rubbish ends up.

Workers clear rubbish from the edge of the Yangtze.

DUMPING GROUND

As well as producing a lot of plastic waste of their own, until January 2018, China received 56 per cent of the world's plastic recycling imports. But the recycling plants were not regulated by the government, and a lot of the plastic that couldn't be recycled would just be dumped in rivers.

To help tackle the issue, China has stopped accepting foreign waste

PROBLEMS WITH PACKAGING

Another significant contributor to plastic pollution in less developed countries are sachets. Many people in Asia and Africa can't afford to buy whole bottles of toiletries such as shampoo. So, brands sell single plastic sachets of products. These sachets are not recyclable, and often end up in the ocean.

RIVER CHIEFS

China has appointed new 'River Chiefs', who are responsible for improving the quality of each river, and reducing the amount of pollution in the water. However, much more drastic changes will be needed around the world to really solve the problem.

MICROPLASTICS

The plastic litter that we can see in our oceans and on our beaches is bad news for the planet. But even worse is the plastic that we can't see: tiny microplastics causing havoc in ocean food chains.

WHAT ARE MICROPLASTICS?

Microplastics are simply pieces of plastic smaller than five millimetres across. Some are created when larger pieces of plastic get broken into small fragments in the ocean. Others are found in toiletries, or come off our clothes when they are washed, and go down the drain (see p 19).

MICROBEADS

Companies add tiny pieces of plastic to products such as face scrubs and toothpastes to increase their cleaning effect. However, these pieces of plastic are too small to be filtered out in water treatment plants, and so end up in rivers and the ocean.

In some countries including the UK, the USA, New Zealand and Canada, products containing microbeads have been banned.

LAUNDRY'S DIRTY SECRET

Laundry is a big source of microplastic pollution. When plastic clothes, particularly items such as fleeces, are cleaned in a washing machine, thousands of tiny plastic fibres get washed off them. Like microbeads, these are too small to be filtered out and so end up in our waterways.

An item of plastic clothing will release more than 700,000 fibres during one wash cycle.

The highest concentration of microplastic pollution in the world has been found in the River Tame in Manchester, UK. It contained more than half a million microplastic particles per square metre.

INTO THE FOOD CHAIN

Once in the ocean, marine animals eat the microplastics, mistaking them for plankton (tiny marine plants and animals) They are then eaten by larger marine animals, and so the plastic travels up the food chain.

Animals such as whales feed on plankton by filtering seawater. But they are consuming microplastics as well.

THE GREAT PACIFIC GARBAGE PATCH

Water in the ocean moves in large circular patterns called gyres, driven by the wind and the rotation of the Earth. Plastic that enters these gyres creates large areas of floating plastic waste. The largest is the Great Pacific Garbage Patch.

The Great Pacific Garbage Patch

Five areas of plastic accumulation in the world's oceans. The biggest is the Great Pacific Garbage Patch.

FACT FILE

Location: The North Pacific Ocean

Size: 1.6 million km², more than three times the size of Spain

Plastic content: 129,000 tonnes approx.

FISHING NETS

Nearly half of the material in the Patch is lost or discarded fishing nets, ropes and other fishing gear. These are sometimes lost accidentally during storms, but they are also deliberately abandoned, as many ports don't have facilities to recycle the nets.

PLASTIC SOUP

The Great Pacific Garbage Patch isn't a floating island of plastic. Instead it's more like a thick soup, with lots of bits of plastic floating within the surface layers of the water. Bigger bits slowly break up into smaller microplastics as they are bashed by waves and bleached by the Sun.

The patch is so big that it would be extremely difficult to clean. It has been estimated that it would take 67 ships one year to clean up less than one per cent of the North Pacific Ocean.

x 67

HENDERSON ISLAND

Plastic doesn't only end up in the water thanks to the ocean currents. Islands that sit within their path, such as Henderson Island in the Pacific, end up drowning in plastic waste. Despite being uninhabited by humans, tiny Henderson island is covered by 18 tonnes of plastic waste which has been washed ashore.

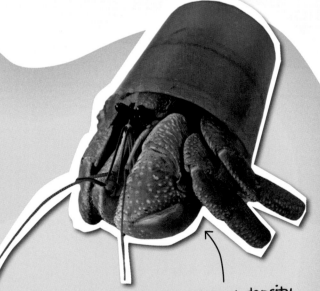

Henderson Island has the highest density of plastic debris anywhere in the world. Hundreds of crabs on the island live in plastic items instead of natural shells.

IMPACTS ON WILDLIFE

Plastic waste in our waterways looks ugly, but for marine creatures it can be deadly. From the tiniest sea creatures to the biggest, marine animals are suffering from the impacts of plastic pollution.

GHOST NETS

Once a fishing boat has dumped its net into the ocean, the net doesn't stop fishing. Fish and other sea creatures get caught in these 'ghost nets', which then attract even more animals that come to scavenge and get caught themselves. And because the nets are made of long-lasting plastic, they can continue killing creatures for decades or even centuries.

The Virginia Institute of Marine Science estimates that abandoned crab pots in Chesapeake Bay, USA, capture 1.25 million blue crabs every year.

ENTANGLEMENT

It isn't just nets that endanger sea creatures. Plastic bags, six-pack can rings and other waste can become wrapped around animals, strangling or injuring them.

TOXIC MICROPLASTIC

A wide range of marine wildlife are accidentally eating microplastics, which is very harmful to their health. Not only does plastic not provide any nutrition, microplastics can be actively toxic. They soak up pollution and dangerous chemicals in the water, which cause disease and affect sea creatures' ability to reproduce.

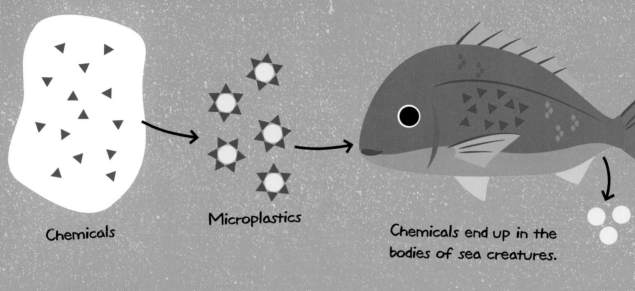

Chemicals

Microplastics

Chemicals end up in the bodies of sea creatures.

Disease-causing chemicals end up in the bodies of small sea creatures. When these sea creatures are eaten by larger creatures, the chemicals end up in their bodies. This is called bioaccumulation.

PLASTIC DIET

As well as being toxic, the sheer amount of plastic being eaten by some sea creatures is enough to be fatal. Leatherback turtles' diet is mainly jellyfish, but they end up eating plastic bags by mistake. Seabirds eat plastic items thinking they are fish, and cannot digest the plastic, so it fills up their stomach and kills them (see pages 24–25).

Around the world, dead whales have been found with their stomachs full of plastic bags and other rubbish.

CASE STUDY: ALBATROSS

Albatrosses are massive seabirds, famous for their size and long flights. But due to their feeding habits, plastic pollution is killing huge numbers of albatross chicks every year.

LIFE AT SEA

The albatross family contains the largest seabirds in the world, the wandering albatross. They have a wingspan of up to 3.5 metres, and have been known to spend as much as five years at sea, without returning to land.

SURFACE FEEDERS

Albatrosses feed mostly by skimming along the surface of the water, catching squid and fish from the upper layer of the sea. This makes them very vulnerable to plastic pollution, as they scoop up a lot of plastic debris, either mistaking it for food, or accidentally catching it along with the sea creatures.

Scientists investigating the effect of ocean plastic on seabirds have found dead birds with hundreds of pieces of plastic in their stomachs.

On Bird Island in the South Atlantic, albatross numbers have halved over the last 35 years.

FACT FILE

Oldest living albatross: Laysan albatross named Wisdom, 67 years

No. of albatross species: 22 – all under threat

No. of critically endangered species: 8

Distribution: Worldwide, especially in the Southern Ocean

CHOKING CHICKS

Adult albatrosses are able to regurgitate pieces of plastic, but chicks are not. The adults take food back to the nest, and accidentally feed their growing young with the plastic pieces. These either cut the chicks' stomachs, fatally injuring them, or it eventually fills them up, until they are unable to eat any proper food, and they die.

ISLAND BREEDERS

Albatrosses don't raise chicks until they are five years old. As albatrosses take such a long time to reach maturity and breed, the death of chicks due to plastic pollution, getting caught on fishing lines and climate change has had a serious impact on their population.

IMPACTS ON HUMANS

Marine wildlife suffers greatly from the impacts of plastic pollution, but what about the effects on humans? As many as 3.5 billion people rely on the sea for their food or their livelihood, so problems in the ocean and waterways affect us, too.

A 2018 study showed that all of the mussels sold in British supermarkets contained microplastics.

PLASTIC IN OUR FOOD

Remember how toxic microplastics make their way up the food chain? In many instances, humans are the top of an ocean food chain, so those toxic plastics are making their way into our food, too. As yet, no large scale studies have been conducted to find out the impact that this might be having on our health. However, we know that other types of pollution have harmful effects, so it is very possible that accidentally consuming microplastics has a health risk.

BPA IN PLASTIC

Another danger is posed by a chemical commonly used in making plastic, Bisphenol A (BPA). It can leach out of plastic containers into our food and drink and studies suggest it can cause health problems.

In the USA and EU, baby bottles must be BPA-free by law.

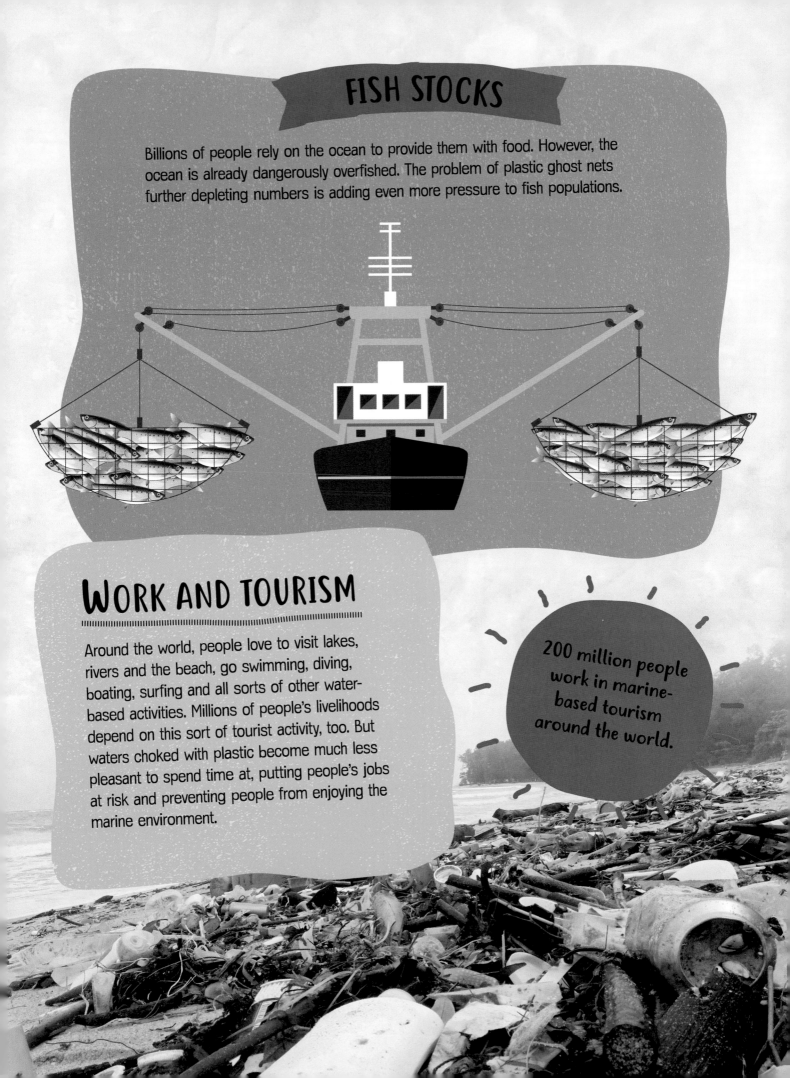

FISH STOCKS

Billions of people rely on the ocean to provide them with food. However, the ocean is already dangerously overfished. The problem of plastic ghost nets further depleting numbers is adding even more pressure to fish populations.

WORK AND TOURISM

Around the world, people love to visit lakes, rivers and the beach, go swimming, diving, boating, surfing and all sorts of other water-based activities. Millions of people's livelihoods depend on this sort of tourist activity, too. But waters choked with plastic become much less pleasant to spend time at, putting people's jobs at risk and preventing people from enjoying the marine environment.

200 million people work in marine-based tourism around the world.

What IS being done?

The plastic crisis can feel insurmountable. But we can turn things around if we all start putting pressure on governments and companies to do things differently, and changing our own behaviour.

UN AGREEMENT

200 countries at a UN assembly have promised to take action on plastic waste. Although the agreement is not legally binding, environmentalists hope that it can be the foundation for a legally binding agreement in the future.

Women using reusable bags and baskets at a local market in Mozambique.

GOVERNMENT ACTION

National governments are putting laws in place to try to stem the tide of single-use plastics. Rwanda, Kenya, Morocco and other African nations have banned plastic bags completely. Other countries are taking measures to limit the number of single-use plastics such as straws, cotton buds and plastic cutlery that are sold.

By 2020, France is aiming to have banned all plastic cups, plates and cutlery.

BUSINESS PRACTICES

Ecologically-aware companies are also beginning to reduce their plastic use. Some cafés and takeaways are replacing their food packaging with 100 per cent compostable containers. Some clothing companies use recycled textiles, while other brands, such as US-based outdoor wear specialist Patagonia, offer a repair service. This means that instead of throwing away a garment when it is worn or damaged, you can send it back to be mended, keeping it out of landfill.

Compostable food containers

SUPERMARKETS

In France, supermarkets are taxed if they use material for packaging which is not easily recyclable. In the Netherlands, a supermarket in Amsterdam has opened offering a plastic-free aisle with 700 products in compostable packaging, while a supermarket chain in New Zealand is launching a plastic-free aisle in each of their stores by 2019.

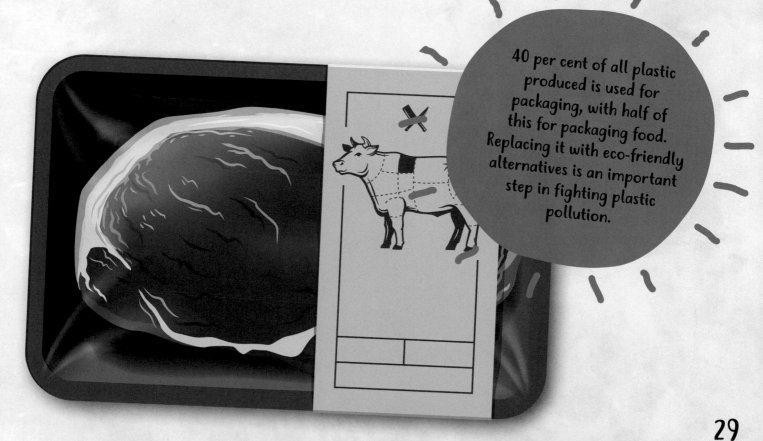

40 per cent of all plastic produced is used for packaging, with half of this for packaging food. Replacing it with eco-friendly alternatives is an important step in fighting plastic pollution.

What CAN you do?

Changing the way the world uses plastic starts with millions of individual acts. By changing our own behaviour, we can start to change the culture of plastic dependence worldwide. Here are some simple things that everyone can do.

REFUSE SINGLE-USE PLASTIC

When you or your family are shopping, look for items that are not packaged in plastic.
If someone tries to give you a plastic bag, a plastic drinking straw or any other single-use plastic item, say you don't want it.

160,000 plastic bags are used globally every second

REDUCE YOUR OVERALL PLASTIC USE

Find out what alternatives there are for the things you normally buy which come in or are made of plastic.
There are hints and tips for plastic-free living on pages 36–39.

Did you know you can buy plastic-free bamboo toothbrushes?

REUSE PLASTIC

If you do have plastic items, make sure to reuse them as many times as possible. For example, if you have some plastic cutlery, keep using it! You don't need to throw it away after a single meal. Reuse any plastic bags or plastic takeaway boxes you already have as many times as you can and, when you have finished with them, make sure to recycle them (see p 32–33).

Plastic straws are used for an average of 20 minutes, then thrown away.

≡ EAT LESS FISH ≡

With half of the plastic in the Great Pacific Garbage Patch being made of abandoned fishing gear, reducing the amount of fish you eat will help address one of the most serious types of ocean pollution.

CAMPAIGN FOR CHANGE

It's important for everyone to take part, but imagine how quickly plastic use would be reduced if the companies who make and sell goods in plastic packaging were responsible for what happened to the plastic once we had finished with it! Check out some tips and ideas on campaigning on page 40–41.

BAN SINGLE-USE PLASTICS **NOW!**

ACT **NOW!**

BAD PLASTIC

RECYCLING PLASTIC

Once you've reused your plastic items as many times as possible, the next most important thing to do is recycle them, instead of throwing them in the bin.

COLLECTION

Depending on where you live, the council or local authority might collect plastic for recycling. Check online to see what they take. However, plastic recycling is patchy, and you might find your council only takes limited types of plastic, or none at all.

Globally, only 9 per cent of plastic is currently recycled.

COMPANIES

If your local council doesn't take plastic for recycling, don't despair! There are many private companies and charities that do. Look online to see if there is anyone doing it in your area. They might even offer a collection service.

Does your school recycle its plastic waste? Speak to your teacher to find out. If not, see if you can convince them to — maybe you could organise a student petition?

A GUIDE TO TYPES OF PLASTIC

Because councils, city authorities and companies will take different types of plastic, look out for the symbols to figure out which items they will accept.

PET 1 or PETE 1

This is the most commonly recycled plastic. It is used for fizzy drink bottles, water bottles and some salad trays.

HDPE 2

Also fairly commonly recycled, this is used to bottle shampoo, cleaning products, bleach and milk.

PVC 3

Less commonly recycled, this is used to make pipes, window and door frames and car parts.

LDPE 4

Also less commonly recycled, this type of plastic is used for things such as carrier bags and plastic films.

PP 5

This is used for items such as margarine tubs and microwave meal trays, as well as being turned into fibres for carpets.

PS 6

Difficult to recycle, this is used for foam takeaway food boxes, protective packaging and insulation.

OTHER 7

Any plastic which doesn't fall into the above categories is given this label. Being difficult to identify, it is not usually recycled.

What about bioplastic?

You might have heard about bioplastics – these are plastics which are made from plants instead of from fossil fuels. But are they any better for the environment?

POLYLACTIC ACID

One of the most common bioplastics is polylactic acid, or PLA. It's made from corn, and is used to make drinks cups, takeaway packaging and other objects. PLA uses less energy to make than traditional plastic, it can be composted and the plants that are used to make it are a renewable resource.

PLA looks a lot like PET plastic, but if a piece of PLA gets mixed up with PET that is being sent for recycling, it ruins the whole batch.

Cups made from PLA

DISADVANTAGES OF PLA

Unfortunately, PLA isn't yet a 'magic bullet' solution to plastic use. We can't replace all our plastic with PLA because it requires huge amounts of land to grow the plants which make it – land which we need to grow food. Also, although PLA is compostable, it only composts in very hot, industrial composters, so if it were dumped in the environment it would still cause pollution.

BIODEGRADABLE PLASTIC

Confusingly, you might see plastic bags and other types of plastic packaging labelled 'biodegradable' or 'oxy-degradable'. These aren't necessarily bioplastics, and while they sound eco-friendly, in practice they may not be. They are designed to break down in the presence of light and oxygen, but they may leave toxic residues behind. In the ocean, the conditions aren't right for them to break down, so they linger on as pollution or break into harmful microplastics.

FUTURE BIOPLASTICS

Scientists are working on new types of bioplastic, and there are some promising developments. Some companies have developed edible bioplastics from a range of natural materials such as seaweed or milk. These bioplastics could be used as food or drink packaging and they wouldn't create any waste – because we can eat them!

Some types of edible packaging for tea or instant noodles would dissolve straight away when they are added to water.

In the future, bioplastics might be made from seaweed.

A PLASTIC-FREE KITCHEN

A huge amount of single-use plastic is used to package food. Reducing our plastic use in this area can have a big, immediate impact. Here are some ideas to help your family move towards a plastic-free kitchen.

Over 500 billion plastic bags are used around the world each year.

BRING BAGS

Take reusable bags with you any time you go shopping. You can get strong reusable plastic bags from the supermarket, or you can use a canvas bag or rucksack. If your family order groceries online, make sure they tick the option to have them delivered without bags.

VEGETABLES

If you get vegetables from the supermarket, choose the ones that are loose, rather than the ones in plastic packets. You don't have to use the plastic bags to put them in. Alternatively, you could see if there is a veg box scheme in your area, as these tend to come without plastic.

DRIED GOODS

Some shops offer a service where you can bring your own container, and they will fill it with rice, pasta or other dried goods. If there isn't a shop like this near you, another option is for your family to buy in bulk. A five or 10 kg bag of rice uses less packaging than the same amount in 500 g bags. Search online for wholesalers in your area.

Take your own containers to the meat or dairy counter in the supermarket. Staff should be happy to use them instead of plastic wrap.

STORING AND CLEANING

Other ways that plastic comes into the kitchen is through the things we use to wash up and to store food. Dish sponges and cloths are often made of plastic — try replacing these with natural loofahs and cotton cloths. Instead of using cling-film to wrap food, look for reusable beeswax-coated cloths.

Loofahs are made from a type of dried fruit.

37

A PLASTIC-FREE BATHROOM

Even better than reusing or recycling plastic is not using it in the first place. As the plastic-free movement gains momentum, it's getting easier to find alternatives. Here's how you can replace plastic in the bathroom.

SHAMPOO AND BODY WASH

The corner of your bath or shower is probably full of plastic bottles containing shampoo, conditioner, body wash and so on. An easy replacement for these is to buy solid versions. Various high street and online shops sell shampoo and conditioner bars which work just as well as the liquid ones.

Did you know you can even get deodorant in bar form? Search online to find ones with many different scents.

CLEAN TEETH

The toothbrushes and toothpaste tubes we use every morning and evening are made from plastic. But there are alternatives. Toothbrushes with bamboo handles are available online, as is toothpaste in glass jars. Most toothbrushes still have plastic bristles, however if you want to go 100 per cent plastic-free you can buy brushes with pig-hair bristles!

REFILLABLES

Another good alternative for cutting down on packaging is to buy refillable products, such as shampoo, laundry detergent, washing-up liquid and so on. Do some research to find out if there are any shops offering refill services near you, and encourage your family to buy from there.

⇒ WET WIPES ⇐

Does your family use a lot of wet wipes? They are mostly made of plastic, and even the ones labelled 'flushable' cause a lot of problems. They can escape the sewer system and enter rivers, where they create pollution, and break up into microplastics. In 2018, over 5,000 wet wipes were found on a 116 square metre stretch of the River Thames in the UK.

WATCH OUT FOR MICROBEADS

Whatever you buy, always remember to watch out for microbeads (see p 18). Some countries have already banned these, but many haven't. They are used in all sorts of products, including toothpastes, scrubs and sun cream. When you go shopping with your family, check ingredients lists, and buy products that use natural alternatives such as ground apricot kernels.

SPREAD THE WORD

Reducing your own plastic use is an important step, but to really solve the problem we all need to work together, and companies need to do things differently, as well as individuals. Here are some ways you can campaign for real change.

PLASTIC-FREE JULY

The plastic-free July campaign began in Australia and has spread to over 150 countries. During July, people try to raise awareness of the plastic crisis, and live plastic-free themselves. Search online for information, hints and tips. By documenting your own plastic-free July on social media, you can encourage others to join in.

You could start your plastic-free month by making a short video about what you are doing, and putting it on social media. Check with an adult first, though.

Why not hold a plastic-free tea party, or a fundraiser with a plastic-free cake stall?

HOST A SCREENING

People are more likely to want to change their behaviour if they can see the effects of plastic pollution themselves. Host a screening of a film such as *Blue Planet II* episode 7, *A Plastic Ocean* by Craig Leeson or online films about microfibres and microbeads from storyofstuff.org.

ASK COMPANIES TO CHANGE

The Ellen MacArthur Foundation has launched the Plastic Pact – an initiative aiming to get brands and governments around the world to move towards a system where all plastic is either compostable, or recovered for reuse. So far the Pact has been launched in the UK and Chile. Why don't you email or write to your favourite brands and ask them to sign up?

With some friends, try writing to a big supermarket chain. Explain that you have been learning about the problem of plastic pollution and ask them to stock more plastic-free products.

ORGANISE A BEACH CLEAN

If you have access to a waterway, why not organise a clean-up? Get a bunch of people together and go armed with bags and gloves. You can make it more fun by playing beach clean bingo. Give everyone a list of plastic items (such as a bottle top, lighter, coke bottle and so on). The first person to collect every item wins a prize!

SCIENTIFIC SOLUTIONS

While we help by reducing our plastic use, scientists around the world are looking for ways to clean up the mass of plastic that we have already produced.

THE OCEAN CLEANUP

The 18-year-old Dutch inventor, Boyan Slat, has invented the 'Ocean Cleanup', a 600-metre-long, three-metre-deep floating 'skirt'. It moves slightly faster than plastic, so after a few months it collects a lot of plastic waste, which can be collected by ship. Because the skirt is solid, sea creatures cannot get entangled in it, making it safe for wildlife.

A section of the floating Ocean Cleanup

The Ocean Cleanup team believe that 60 floating skirts could clean 50 per cent of the Great Pacific Garbage Patch in five years.

PLASTIC TO FUEL

Technologies such as pyrolysis and gasification heat plastic to very high temperatures and break it down into a type of oil that can be used as fuel. This has the advantage that it can stop plastic becoming pollution, and can even use up plastic that is already in landfill. However, the fuel that is produced does still release carbon dioxide when burned, which contributes to climate change.

ROADS MADE OF PLASTIC

In 2006 Indian chemistry professor, Dr R Vasudevan, developed a way of adding shredded waste plastic to the tar that is used to build roads. The mixture of plastic and tar makes the roads stronger, and more resistant to weathering. In 2015, the Indian government announced that the default material for new roads should be the plastic mix.

Every kilometre of plastic-mix road uses one million plastic bags, and costs 8 per cent less than a regular road.

PLASTIC-EATING BACTERIA

In 2016, scientists from Japan discovered a type of bacteria which can eat PET plastic (see p 33). The bacteria produces an enzyme (a type of protein which speeds up chemical reactions) that breaks the plastic down. It isn't effective enough yet to be a solution to the plastic crisis, but scientists are working on ways to make the enzyme more efficient.

GLOSSARY

bioaccumulation the process where toxic substances build up in a food chain. Plants take up small amounts of toxic substances. The plants are eaten by small animals, and the toxic substances transfer to their bodies. This continues up the food chain

biodegradable able to be broken down by natural organisms such as bacteria and fungi

bioplastic a plastic made from recently-grown plant material

BPA a chemical that is used in making certain plastics, and may have harmful effects on human health

camphor a waxy solid that comes from the camphor laurel tree

catalyst a substance that sets off a chemical reaction

celluloid a transparent and flammable plastic film

cellulose the main substance found in plant cell walls, it helps plants stay stiff and strong

climate change a change in weather patterns and temperatures around the world, caused by human activity

debris scattered pieces of rubbish or broken-up material

decompose to rot down

enzyme a substance produced by a living organism that acts as a catalyst

food chain the order in which living things eat one another, starting with plants and ending with large predators

fossil fuel a fuel such as oil or coal that was formed over millions of years from the remains of plants and animals

gasification a process that turns waste into a gas for fuel

greenhouse gas a gas in our atmosphere that traps heat from the Sun and contributes to climate change

gyre a large circular system of ocean currents

import bring goods or other materials and objects into a country

insurmountable too big to overcome

ivory the hard, creamy material that makes up the tusks of elephants and some other mammals

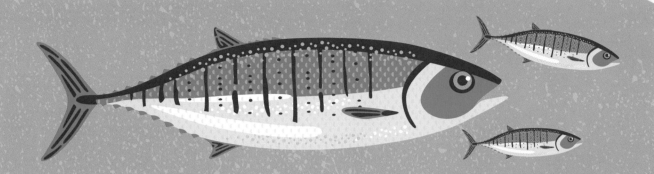

leach a process by which chemicals are removed from a material such as plastic and end up elsewhere

microbead a small piece of plastic added to products such as toiletries to aid cleaning

microplastic a tiny fragment of plastic

molecule the smallest unit of a substance that has all the properties of that substance

overfishing taking fish out of the ocean faster than they can reproduce, lowering population numbers

oxy-degradable breaks down in the presence of oxygen

particle a very small piece of something

pollution the presence in the environment of substances or objects that are harmful

polymer a substance made of long chains of molecules joined together

polymerisation the process where molecules join together to make polymers

property a characteristic of a substance

pyrolysis a process that breaks down materials at high temperatures

regurgitate to bring swallowed food up again

residue a small amount of something that gets left behind

single-use an object such as a plastic straw that is designed to be used once, then thrown away

synthetic man-made

toxic harmful to health

versatility ability to be used for lots of different functions or activities

weathering wearing away after being exposed to the atmosphere

FURTHER READING

BOOKS

This Book is Not Rubbish: 50 Ways to Ditch Plastic, Reduce Rubbish and Save the World!

By Isabel Thomas (Wren & Rook, 2018)
Find 50 practical tips to ditch plastic and help the environment in this book

Recycling and Reusing (Discover Through Craft)
By Louise Spilsbury (Franklin Watts, 2017)

Explore how plastic (and other materials) can be recycled and reused in a selection of fun craft activities.

No. More. Plastic.:
What you can do to make a difference – the #2minutesolution

By Martin Dorey (Ebury Press, 2018)
Author Martin Dorey started the #2minutebeachclean movement. This book explores more ways to stop the tide of ocean plastic.

Caring for the Environment (I'm a Global Citizen)
By Georgia Amson-Bradshaw (Franklin Watts, 2019)

What other pressures are there on the natural world? How could we be doing things differently to take better care of the planet? This book looks at some of the problems and solutions.

⇒ WEBSITES ⇐

There are lots of organisations taking action against plastic pollution. Check some of them out here.

www.plasticfreejuly.org

Find hints and tips for living plastic-free.

www.plasticpollutioncoalition.org

This is the website of a coalition of over 700 organisations that are working to reduce the problem of plastic pollution.

www.sas.org.uk

UK-based Surfers Against Sewage is a grassroots organisation working to clean up the seas, making the water better for humans and wildlife.

⇒ WATCH ⇐

Albatross by Chris Jordan

A beautiful and heart-wrenching film about the impact of plastic pollution on albatrosses that live in the North Pacific. It can be viewed online here: **www.albatrossthefilm.com**

All the Way to the Ocean by Freedom Free Publishing

This animated story of two best friends shows the relationship between cities' storm drains and the ocean. Find it at **www.youtube.com/watch?v=sZW2ByM623g**

A Plastic Ocean by Craig Leeson

This full-length documentary shows the extent of plastic pollution in our oceans.

A Plastic Ocean 40
albatrosses 24–25

Baekeland, Leo 8, 10–11
Bakelite 8, 10–11
bamboo toothbrushes 34
beach clean 41
biodegradable plastic 9, 35
bioplastic 34–35
Blue Planet 40
BPA 26

carbon dioxide 7, 42
China 14, 16–17
climate change 7, 24, 42
compostable 29, 34, 41
crude oil 6, 7

edible plastic 35

fish 5, 22, 23, 25, 27, 31
fishing gear 20, 22, 31
fundraisers 40

gasification 42
Great Pacific Garbage Patch
   20–21, 31
gyres 20

Henderson Island 21

Kevlar 9

landfill 13, 14, 29
laundry 18, 19
loofahs 39

microbeads 18, 37, 40
microplastics 18–19, 21, 23,
   26, 35, 37

NASA 13
nurdles 6
nylon 9

Ocean Cleanup 42
overfishing 27

pig bristles 13, 36
PLA 34
plastic
   ban 28
   Pact 41
   roads 43
plastic-eating bacteria 43
Plastic-Free July 40

polymers 6
pyrolysis 42

recycling 14, 15, 17, 29,
   32–33, 34, 35
refillables 37
River Tame 19
River Thames 37

sachets 17
shellac 10
solid shampoo 36

tourism 27

United Nations 28

wet wipes 37
wildlife 5, 19, 21, 22–23,
   24–25, 26

Yangtze river 16–17